BRITAIN IN OLD PHOTOGRAPHS

LEEDS
IN THE NEWS

BRETT HARRISON

Budding
BOOKS

First published in 1996 by
Sutton Publishing Limited

This edition first published in 2001 by Budding
Books, an imprint of Sutton Publishing Limited

British Library Cataloguing in Publication Data
A catalogue record for this book is available from the
British Library.

ISBN 1 84015 198 6

Typeset in 10/12 Perpetua.
Typesetting and origination by
Sutton Publishing Limited.
Printed in Great Britain by
J.H. Haynes & Co., Sparkford.

Dedication
To Edith Waite

CONTENTS

FOREWORD

Leeds has a long and fascinating history, much of which can be found in the rich collections of archives held by the West Yorkshire Archive Service which has been used to compile this fascinating book. The Leeds District Archives alone holds over three miles of records, dating from the twelfth to the twentieth centuries, which have accrued over a period of more than fifty years.

Leeds is proud of its tradition of caring for the archives, not only of the City, but also of the Metropolitan District and of a wider region of Yorkshire. When figures were first kept, in 1958, 215 people used the Archives. By 1995 this had grown to nearly three thousand.

This tradition began with the Leeds City Council in 1938, and developed further in 1982 with the setting up of joint arrangements for archives. At this time the five Metropolitan District Councils of Bradford, Calderdale, Kirklees, Leeds and Wakefield joined with the former West Yorkshire County Council to form the county-wide West Yorkshire Archive Service. This has brought many advantages, including access to specialist facilities such as information technology, microfilming and conservation, which would be expensive to set up separately. There are also other, less immediately obvious, benefits from joint arrangements. A great deal of material relating to the Leeds District forms part of the county-wide collections at the Archive Service's Headquarters at Wakefield. As part of the Joint Archive Service, Leeds is involved in the administration and management of these records, which cannot be split up, but which are also a very important part of Leeds's archival heritage.

Brett Harrison is a professional archivist who has worked at the Leeds District Archives since 1982. He has seen the potential in the vast collection of photographs taken by Jimmie Waite which now forms part of the holdings of the Archive Service's Leeds office. He is to be congratulated on his selection, which shows a fine variety of people and scenes, with a fair sprinkling of celebrities, disasters, sporting triumphs and observations of everyday life, all of which go to make up *Leeds in the News*.

Councillor G.B. Midwood
Chairman, West Yorkshire
Joint Services Committee, Archives,
Archaeology and Trading Standards Sub-Committee

INTRODUCTION

This book celebrates the survival of a significant archive of photographic negatives belonging to Photopress (Leeds) Ltd, a firm founded by Jimmie Waite. Now held by the West Yorkshire Archive Service, Leeds, at Sheepscar, the whole collection consists of over 67,000 glass and film negatives, most of which were taken between 1958 and 1974. Photopress was involved in an extensive range of work, including wedding, passport, commercial and freelance press photography. The press work covered not only Leeds but extended throughout the old West Riding of Yorkshire, from Doncaster in the south to York in the north.

In the daily process of capturing images that would appeal to newspaper picture editors the photographers consumed thousands of plates and rolls of film. Each event was recorded by a variety of images with only one or part of one, perhaps, being worth printing and despatching to a newspaper. The archive includes them all. Therefore, some of the images in this book may well have appeared in print before but many have not. Also included in this compilation are some prints from Jimmie Waite's own collection dating from 1935 to 1958. The majority of photographs here, however, consist of new prints from the old negatives. Many prints were specially commissioned, but without the business files it is difficult now to identify them. In the main an attempt has been made to include the images that resulted from photocalls where the subject wanted publicity for an event.

Additionally there are chance photographs recording particular occasions, whether the scene of a fire or an accident, or a sporting event. What unites them all is the skill of the professional photographer, a craft perhaps undervalued by the 'man in the street'. This craft required a total familiarity with the capacities of the various press cameras, an ability to frame a moment in time and process the result in minutes to make the next edition of a newspaper. As Beaumont Newhall observed in *The History of Photography* (1982), 'Although the technique of the news photographer does not differ from that of any other cameraman, the special demands made on his skill, daring and ingenuity in getting unusual pictures, and the need of turning out a print with all possible speed, make his work a special branch.' Such photographers were under constant pressure to get the image to the newspaper while the story was still newsworthy. Missing a deadline meant the photograph was worthless.

The best results are images that live in the memory. The initial selection of pictures was carried out on the basis of bald index entries rather than images, and the result has been quite revealing. Leeds emerges, particularly in the 1960s, as a city growing in self-confidence, but changing under the social pressures that were affecting the country as a whole. Large-scale private investment in city centre developments, such as shopping centres and office blocks, was matched by a drastic remodelling of the road system by the municipal authorities. The 'Leeds Approach' to the traffic problems of the future brought the first stages of the Inner Ring Road, an improvement in bus mobility and an attempt to restrict access for private cars to the city centre. Major rehousing projects led to the demolition of thousands of Victorian back-to-back houses and the barrack-like Quarry Hill flats, and the construction of blocks of high-rise flats and community shopping centres. New high-rise office blocks also flourished in the city centre, creating a cityscape which has only recently begun to be refashioned.

In other areas of city life as well, most particularly in sport, Leeds has demonstrated a fresh vigour. Yorkshire County Cricket Club won the Championship regularly, while Leeds United Football Club climbed out of the Second Division to reach the top of the First Division many times, winning the Football League and the Fairs Cup in 1968, and the FA Cup in 1972. Leeds Rugby League team won the League Championship for the first time for sixty years in 1960.

Economic forces were redrawing the social map of Leeds. The majority of people in the city were better housed, better educated and healthier. Unemployment remained low in the 1950s and '60s and was a factor in the encouragement of immigration from the Caribbean and the Indian sub-continent. The long-term trend in employment has seen a decline in the numbers of people working in manufacturing and a steady increase in employment in the service sector. This has been particularly noticeable in the development of financial services. But another area of growth has been in the radio and television industries; 1968 was a significant year with the coming of BBC Television to Woodhouse Lane and Yorkshire TV to Kirkstall Road. Radio Leeds also began broadcasting from the new Merrion Centre.

While cinemas, theatres and newspapers closed under the impact of television there was growth in other forms of leisure activity. Improved sports facilities, bingo halls, bowling alleys and ice-rinks appeared in the 1960s along with discotheques and nightclubs.

Symbolic of what was happening to the city was the career of its most famous personality. Jimmy Savile, a former Leeds coal-miner who established himself as one of the country's first disc jockeys in the 1960s, went on to become a leading television personality in the '70s and '80s. The photographs in this compilation may be seen as a reflection of the vibrancy of this period in the history of the city.

'Beatlemania' arrives in Leeds: fans in the audience at the Odeon, Leeds, at the Beatles concert on 3 November 1963.

JAMES WAITE AND PHOTOPRESS (LEEDS) LTD, 1912–1982

Jimmie Waite (1912–82), photographed in 1962. Jimmie left Leeds Modern School in 1928 with no clear idea of any future career, and had a couple of jobs before going into photography. His sister Grace and her husband, Roy Sunderland, introduced him to Bob Ledbetter, who ran a press agency, and Jimmie was taken on as a trainee. He found the job stimulating and enjoyed press photography.

By the outbreak of war he had become a partner in the firm Ledbetters/Leeds Press Agency but after war service he decided to set up on his own. A born entrepreneur, he soon developed a wide network of contacts and built up a considerable business. Sometime in 1949 he opened Photopress (Leeds) at 26 East Parade. When the building was scheduled for demolition he was forced to find new premises and moved to 16 New Station Street in 1960. There he registered the firm as a limited company and Photopress (Leeds) Ltd was incorporated on 23 March 1962. With the opening of the new Merrion Centre in 1964, Jimmie became one of the first tenants. From 1968 he faced growing competition and the first symptoms of Parkinson's Disease appeared, but he struggled bravely on until 1976, when the business closed.

35

LEEDS COLLEGE OF TECHNOLOGY

CLASS ENTRY FORM

CLASS No. *P 52*

SUBJECT *Pure Photography*

NAME (*in FULL*) *James Waite*

Address *75 Monkbridge Dr. Meanwood*

Age *23*   Occupation *Press Photographer*

Employer's Name *R.B. Ledbetter*

Address *8 Oxford Row, Leeds*

STATE IF FEE IS PAID BY EMPLOYER (Yes, or No) *No*

Other classes taken this session, including those taken at other Colleges or Schools :—

Class No.	Subject	Evening
P.54	*Pure Photography*	*WED.*

Fees Receipt No. *4 58*
    or
Admission Ticket No.
    or
W.R.C.C. Exhibition No.

DECLARATION

I declare that it is my intention to attend regularly, to do the work prescribed for the Class, to sit for the examination if required and in all respects to comply with the rules of the College.

Signature *J. Waite*   Date *26/9/35*

James Waite's entry form for an evening course run by Leeds College of Technology on Pure Photography in 1935. The course was designed for both amateur and professional photographers and concentrated on the technical aspects of photography. Other courses were run on the chemistry and physics aspects. (By kind permission of Leeds Metropolitan University)

East Parade, 29 July 1937. From 1949 to 1961 the Photopress (Leeds) office was at no. 26, the brick building in the centre. Reception was on the third floor and the dark room, processing areas and offices were on the fourth floor. The local offices of the *Daily Mail* and the *News Chronicle* were conveniently in the same building. From these premises Jimmie operated as a press photographer, freelancing for local newspapers, particularly the *Yorkshire Evening News*, and working for the police and solicitors, as well as for commercial firms. He also worked in the competitive wedding business. When the firm moved, some 4,500 glass negatives were left behind in the building.

New Station Street, May 1962. Looking towards Leeds City station with the Photopress shop on the right at no. 16, this photograph was taken to illustrate the problems being created for the firm by car parking. It also shows the offices of the *Daily Mail* next door, the *Daily Express* next door but one, and the *News of the World* across the road. The new Photopress office had less space but was very convenient for the station for sending prints to Manchester for the northern editions of national newspapers.

Smash and grab at Photopress (Leeds) Ltd, 16 New Station Street, 19 August 1961. The shop had diversified into selling middle-of-the-range cameras, film and equipment. No camera cost more than £30.

The Photopress (Leeds) shop at 12/14 Merrion Centre, 3 June 1965. Conditions were a lot better in these up-to-date premises. There was a small studio for passport photographs which was soon enlarged to add depth for additional lighting and focus for portraits. Susan Waite, Jimmie's eldest daughter, took over responsibility for window-dressing, which she enjoyed.

SECTION TWO

PHOTOGRAPHERS

Robert 'Bob' Ledbetter in 1985, aged 85, pictured with a 9 x 12 VN press camera. He had been interested in photography from the age of nine and while working in the advertisement department of the Yorkshire Post *he became friendly with the process engraver who also acted as photographer. At the age of twenty-three he decided to become a freelance press photographer. His firm became one of the best-known in Yorkshire, eventually specializing in weddings. Jimmie Waite trained under him and became a partner in Ledbetters / Leeds Press Agency before the Second World War. Bob retired in 1967. (Photograph by courtesy of Winpenny Photography, Otley)*

Photographers at a football match, possibly at Elland Road in the early 1950s. Left to right: Dennis Flatt (*Bradford Telegraph and Argus*), Dennis Dobson (*Yorkshire Post*), Jimmie Waite (*Photopress (Leeds)*), Frank Carlill (*Yorkshire Evening News*), Henry Mconomy (freelance). Conditions were not always ideal. Photographers covered the goal being attacked by the local team, and sat behind the goal to get a good shot. Jimmie was especially at home at sporting events of all kinds.

Arthur Thompson, the *Daily Mail*'s northern photographer, celebrated his sixty-fifth birthday in the Victoria Hotel, Great George Street on 16 November 1957. He was also celebrating fifty years as a press photographer, and the occasion was photographed by Jimmie. Thompson trained on the *Leeds Mercury* and was one of the best-known and most talented press photographers in the north of England. He was awarded the BEM. Top row, left to right: Paul Hines (*Yorkshire Evening Echo*), Herbert Dewhirst, chief photographer (*Yorkshire Evening Post*), Alan Cussins (*Yorkshire Post*, Bradford), Dennis Dobson (*Yorkshire Post*, Leeds), Eddie Holland (*Yorkshire Post*, Leeds), Frank Newbold (Ackrills, Harrogate), George Williamson (Photopress (Leeds)). Middle row: Wilbur Wright (*Yorkshire Post*, Hull), George Bennett (*Yorkshire Evening Post*), Edward Winpenny (*Yorkshire Evening Post*, Leeds), Jack Tordoff (*Yorkshire Evening Post*, Leeds), Arthur Thompson, holding an MPP Technical or Speed Graphic press camera, Laurie Mercer (*Yorkshire Evening Post*, Leeds), George Stott (*Yorkshire Post*, York). Front row: Dennis Richmond (*Yorkshire Evening News*, Leeds), Irving Crawford (*Yorkshire Evening News*, Leeds), Jack Hickes (*Yorkshire Evening News*, Leeds), Ronnie Newbould (*Yorkshire Evening News*), Arthur Benson (*Yorkshire Evening Post*, Leeds), Jack Slater (*Yorkshire Evening News*, Leeds).

Ernest Ward, captain of England's rugby league team, being photographed with the match ball at Headingley, 10 November 1950. The match was played between England and France for the Jean Galia trophy. England won by 14 points to 9. The photographers are, left to right: Roger Cross (*Daily Mail*), Edmund Dewhirst (freelance), -?-, Jimmie Waite.

Prime Minister Harold Macmillan grouse-shooting on the moors at Masham, 15 August 1957. The photographers are, left to right: John Varley (*Daily Mirror*), Edmund Dewhirst (freelance, ex-*News Chronicle*), Mike Briggs (Photopress), -?-, Arthur Thompson (*Daily Mail*), Arthur Benson (*Yorkshire Evening Post*), Jimmie Waite (Photopress).

THE EARLY YEARS

Jimmie Waite posing in his aerial photography kit in front of a De Havilland DH60 Gipsy Moth, c. 1942. Jimmie grew up in Meanwood where he met a local girl, Edith Woodward, in 1934. They were engaged the following year and married in 1938. He became a partner in Ledbetters by 1939 but was then called up. He joined the Royal Navy and went to the photographic school at Portsmouth in 1941 and then to the Fleet Air Arm photographic school at Ford. After that he worked on aircraft recognition and undertook further training in Yarmouth, Nova Scotia, in April 1943.

Bertram Woodward with his wife Alice and their children Valerie, Geoffrey and Edith at home at 3 Oddy Fold, Parkside Road, Meanwood, December 1936. This photograph is a good example of the use of a 'sashalite' flash.

Edith Waite with her friend, Eva Heaton, on the River Wharfe at Collingham, in the summer of 1939.

The issue of gas masks provided the opportunity for many comic pictures. This one shows Edith Waite and her sister, Valerie Woodward, ready for tennis and a gas attack in 1939!

Jimmie Waite wearing his gas mask and holding a VN (Van Neck) 9 x 12 press camera, 1939.

'Bright young things' at the Capitol Ballroom, Meanwood, *c.* 1938. Jimmie Waite is second from the left and Edith Woodward is second from the right.

Proud father Jimmie Waite took this portrait of his daughter Susan as the May Queen at Talbot Road County Primary School in 1946.

Sub-Lieutenant James Waite of the Fleet Air Arm, 1945. He had successfully applied for a commission and was demobbed in Ceylon in March 1946. He took the opportunity to see more of the world on his voyage home.

Mrs Edith Waite in ARP ambulance driver's uniform on her first day of service soon after the outbreak of war. It was an excellent photographic opportunity . . . and the *Daily Sketch* duly took it.

SATURDAY, SEPTEMBER 23, 1939.—Page 5.

inks He a U-boat

With Her Knitting On Her Back

'HARD LUCK, MATE'—*WOMAN TO GERMAN PRISONER*

'NOT SO HARD'

—HE REPLIED

GERMAN prisoners of war have begun to arrive in England.

This statement is made by the Ministry of Information in a communiqué, which states that a number of German officers arrived yesterday

They were taken to a prison camp, while other German prisoners were taken to another camp.

Their arrival was seen by very few people, and those who did see them created no demonstration. Indeed, some of the prisoners laughed when a woman in a small group of spectators at a station shouted "Hard luck, mate." One of the prisoners replied, "Not so hard."

CITY PARKS MAY BE VEGETABLE PLOTS

Latest war-time proposals in Glasgow include the erection of eight 5,000-gallon water tanks in various districts for fire-fighting and large-scale cultivation of vegetables in the city parks.

The tanks are to be in areas where normal supplies might be difficult if many fires broke out during an air raid.

The vegetables would be supplied to hospitals and also disposed of through ordinary trade channels.

There'll be no time wasted by this Leeds ambulance driver. Peeping out of her knapsack as she goes on duty is her knitting. The girl on the left makes her gas mask box serve as a beauty box as well. Concealed in the lid is a mirror.

The *Daily Sketch*, 23 September 1939.

Susan Waite in a dolly tub, 1946. You can almost see the headline 'Phew, wot a scorcher!'.

Life must go on. This specially posed photograph, possibly taken by Bob Ledbetter, shows bomb damage after an air raid in 1941 or 1942, somewhere in north Leeds. Notice the typical Anderson shelter in the foreground.

An official inspection of bomb damage at 7–10 Cardigan Road, Headingley, after the air raid on 8 August 1942. The bombs damaged or destroyed 130 houses in this part of Headingley. Leeds was more fortunate than most of the large British cities, enduring only nine air raids and suffering only 77 fatalities; in contrast, there were 82 air raids on Hull, where 1,205 people were killed.

King George VI, Queen Elizabeth and the Princess Royal photographed in the Civic Hall during a visit to Leeds, 21 October 1937. Standing, left to right: Sir Samuel Hoare, the Countess Spencer, Tom Coombs (lord mayor of Leeds), Lord Harewood, the Hon. Piers Legh, Mrs Coombs (the lady mayoress), Mr Alan Lascelles, Thomas Thornton (town clerk). Jimmie must have assisted Bob Ledbetter on this picture – although the *Yorkshire Post* claimed it as an exclusive, the print is clearly stamped Leeds Press Agency.

WEDDINGS

*The comedian Spike Milligan and his new wife, singer
Patricia Ridgway, outside Rawdon Catholic Church, 28
April 1962. This was a major media event because of the
enormous success of the 'Goon Show' which had begun in
1951 and ended after 200 episodes in January 1960.
Milligan invented nearly all the characters, wrote most of
the material and performed many of the characters, but the
strain brought mental breakdown and wrecked his first
marriage. Weddings were the staple diet of professional
photographers. It was the custom for a number of
photographers to compile a selection of prints and submit
them for the couple to choose the best. This resulted in some
gentle sabotage, such as Vaseline smeared on the lens, if a
camera was left unguarded for a second.*

Harry Secombe signing autographs at Spike Milligan's wedding. They had first met in the North African desert and teamed up in the 'Goon Show'. Secombe played the character of Ned Seagoon alongside Peter Sellers and, for the first year, Michael Bentine.

Jack Hickes recorded the photographers present at Spike Milligan's wedding. Back row, left to right: John Heath (Ledbetters), Brian Worsnop (West Riding News Service, Huddersfield), John Varley (*Daily Mirror*, Leeds), Jack Tordoff (*Yorkshire Post*), Jimmie Waite, Dennis Dobson (*Daily Mail*, Leeds). Front row: -?-, David Hickes (Photopress (Leeds)), Harry Fletcher (*Yorkshire Evening Post*), Barry Wilkinson (*Bradford Telegraph and Argus*), -?-. (Photograph courtesy of Jack Hickes Photography)

The wedding scene for the film *This Sporting Life*, starring Rachel Roberts as Margaret Hammond and Colin Blakely as Maurice Braithwaite, took place at Drighlington Church, 21 May 1962. The Photopress photographer, Mike Briggs, went along to play the role of wedding photographer, and when he saw the finished film was upset to find he had been left on the cutting-room floor.

A circus wedding at Holy Trinity church, Boar Lane, 14 January 1962. The chimpanzee trainer, Danny Ashcroft, married Joan Burnall, a circus showgirl.

Policewoman Inspector Gillian Greenbank
and Police Inspector Alan Kenneth Stoneley
after their wedding at Leeds Register
Office, listening to a message of
congratulations over the walkie-talkie held
by Policewoman Sergeant Evelyn Ingham,
18 January 1969.

Student nurse Barbara Judith Waterhouse married theatre technician Alex J. Richardson at Leeds Register
Office on 3 January 1970. They both worked at Leeds General Infirmary. Jimmy Savile, disc jockey,
television personality and charity worker, acted as the bride's chauffeur, driving his own Rolls-Royce.

Albert Johanneson, who played outside left for Leeds United, married Norma Comrie at Blenheim Baptist Church, 27 February 1963. He came from South Africa in 1961 as one of Don Revie's first signings and was a key member of the successful team that took Leeds into the First Division in 1964.

Welterweight boxer Jeff Gale (aged 19) and Jacquie Foster (aged 17) were married at St Peter's Church, Bramley, on 13 October 1973. His friend, Joe Bugner (right), European heavyweight boxing champion, was the best man.

PORTRAITS AND PASSPORTS

A studio portrait of the actor and Leeds city councillor,
Bernard Atha, 10 July 1963. At this time, he was
standing as the Labour parliamentary candidate for Pudsey
and needed a photograph for his election leaflets. He went
on to use the portrait in local election material and
business publicity.
It was not until Photopress took over the premises at the
Merrion Centre that Jimmie was able to consider extending
the work of his firm to include passport and portrait
photography. The move coincided with the gradual
shrinkage in the market for press photographs. The
Yorkshire Evening News *closed in December 1963, and*
there were fewer editions of other local and national
newspapers as a result of growing competition from
television. The northern offices of many national
newspapers closed in the late 1960s.

Retired bank manager Eric Empsall of Leeds
needed a passport for a cruise to Norway. This
photograph, taken on 12 January 1971,
illustrates how the sitter's identity was
protected in case the photographers got the
negatives confused.

Bill Connor, Archivist to the National Register
of Archives, West Riding (Northern Section)
Committee, now Principal District Archivist,
Leeds District Archives. He simply needed a
photograph to renew his passport on
22 September 1970.

SECTION SIX

ROYAL VISITS

*Queen Mary entering Temple Newsam House, followed by
Lord Harewood, and being greeted by the lord and lady
mayoress of Leeds (Alderman and Mrs R.H. Blackburn), 28
August 1933. The Queen had asked to revisit the house
where she had stayed in 1894, when she and her husband
had been guests of Mrs Meynell Ingram. Royal visits to
Leeds could always be relied upon to provide good
photographs for all the local newspapers and the
photographers turned out in large numbers. Members of the
Royal family with Yorkshire connections were most
commonly seen at significant events.*

Princess Margaret at St James's Hospital, Leeds, 3 July 1954. She had been presenting medals, prizes and certificates to student nurses. She was wearing a heavy silk dress with an accordion-pleated skirt, patterned with mauve green-stemmed flowers.

Robert Menzies, the Australian prime minister, after receiving the honorary degree of Doctor of Laws at Leeds University, 22 March 1961. He was photographed with the Chancellor of the University, the Princess Royal, and her page. The Princess Royal was the only daughter of King George V and Queen Mary. She married Viscount Lascelles in 1922 and moved into Harewood House in 1930, when her husband succeeded to the title as 6th Earl of Harewood.

The Duke of Edinburgh talked to the crowd after opening the Martin Wing and Link Block laboratories at Leeds General Infirmary on 3 November 1961. With him were the lord mayor and lady mayoress, Alderman and Mrs P. Woodward, Sir George Martin and Sir Charles Morris, Vice-Chancellor of the University of Leeds.

Policemen leaving the Central police station in the Municipal Buildings to go on duty for the visit of the Duke of Edinburgh to Leeds, 3 November 1961. The town hall is in the background. Leeds City Police moved into their new headquarters in Brotherton House, Westgate, in April 1965.

The Duchess of Kent is the only daughter of Sir William Worsley of Hovingham. She married the Duke of Kent in June 1961 and was called upon to undertake many official duties after the death of the Princess Royal in 1965. Here she is presenting awards to nurses at Leeds General Infirmary on 10 March 1967 and afterwards posed for the photographers.

The Duchess of Kent at Leeds University's Brotherton Library, 10 March 1967. She succeeded the Princess Royal as Chancellor of the University in May 1966.

Lord Snowdon at Richmond Machine Tool Co. Ltd, 28 October 1965. He was visiting the city as adviser to the Council of Industrial Design and had been guest of honour at the *Yorkshire Post* literary luncheon as a co-author of *Private View*, an illustrated study of British art and of London as a world art centre.

The Duchess of Kent opened Yorkshire Television's headquarters in Kirkstall Road on 29 July 1968. Also present was Sir Richard Graham, chairman of the company. The £5 million studio centre was the first in the country designed for full colour capability.

CELEBRITIES AND POLITICIANS

Gracie Fields, aged 70, photographed on 30 November 1968 with her husband Boris, in City Square, Leeds. The famous singer and filmstar had come out of retirement to perform at Batley Variety club. There were many photo calls and personal appearances by singers, actors and politicians over the years but few actually made the newspapers. They had to have a touch of originality to appeal to picture editors and even then they could be ditched in favour of some topical news picture. During the sixties Batley Variety club attracted many international show business stars by offering generous fees and providing customers with high-class entertainment in a nightclub environment. Many of the star entertainers came to Leeds and Bradford Airport on their way to Batley.

Prime Minister Neville Chamberlain outside Lord Swinton's house at Swinton, Masham, on 30 December 1937. He had been a regular visitor here since 1921. Also in the group are Hon. John and the Hon. Philip Cunliffe-Lister, Major the Hon. Edward Cadogan, Major and Mrs Turner, Miss MacSwinney and Miss Hannay, with Lord and Lady Swinton on the right. This was another Leeds Press Agency picture that appeared in the *Yorkshire Post*.

Judy Garland photographed signing autographs backstage at the Odeon, The Headrow, on 15 October 1960. She was in Leeds for 'An Evening with Judy Garland', her two-hour song marathon, which she performed on Sunday 16 October as part of a provincial tour following her West End appearances.

Sir Arthur Bliss, Master of the Queen's Music, was a judge for the 1st Leeds International Pianoforte Competition at Queens Hall, 18 September 1963. Established by Fanny Waterman, this triennial event has become a huge success.

The actor Peter Ustinov with his Hispano-Suiza car at Roundhay Park Mansion, 20 April 1962. He was appearing with Diana Wynyard at the Grand Theatre, Leeds, in his new play *Photo Finish* before taking the play to London.

Pat Phoenix (Elsie Tanner in *Coronation Street*) officially opened shops at the new Lincoln Green Shopping Centre, 3 November 1962. This was one of a planned series of small local shopping centres around the city built to serve areas that had undergone redevelopment.

The Beatles – John Lennon, George Harrison, Paul McCartney and Ringo Starr – in the dressing-room of the Odeon, Leeds, on their second visit on 3 November 1963. They played to a capacity audience of 2,500 – with another 8,000 fans outside. Also on the bill were the Vernons Girls, Brook Brothers, Peter Jay and the Jaywalking Rockmen, and the Kestrel vocal group. The compère was Frank Berry, a comedian from Canada.

Ringo Starr on the drum kit of Peter Jay and the Jaywalking Rockmen, backstage at the Odeon on Sunday 3 November 1963.

The Bachelors, the popular singing group, visited Vallances on 13 August 1964. They flew in to Leeds and Bradford Airport from Blackpool to sign copies of their new release. Formed in Dublin in 1958 as a folk group, it featured the brothers Conleth and Declan Cluskey, and John Stokes. They had their first Top Ten hit with *Charmaine* in the summer of 1963.

P.J. Proby, the pop singer, performed at Leeds town hall on 5 March 1965. Born James Marcus Smith in Houston, Texas, he came over to the UK in 1963 and reached number 3 in the Top Ten with *Hold Me*. Later that year he was banned by both ABC and BBC television because of his tendency to split his velvet trousers in live performances!

Harold Wilson, MP and Labour opposition leader, addressed an election campaign meeting in Leeds town hall on 8 February 1964. Denis Healey, MP for Leeds North East, was at his side. Wilson won the election in October and formed a government with an overall majority of only four seats.

Eden Kane, the pop singer, made a personal appearance at the Silver Blades skating rink, Kirkstall, on 14 May 1965. Born Richard Sarstedt, he won a talent contest in 1960 and had a number 1 hit with *Well I Ask You*. He followed this up with more hits in 1962 and reached the Top Ten again with *Boys Cry* in 1964.

Jayne Mansfield, the Hollywood film star, was photographed on 30 April 1967 at Armley Gaol before going on to perform at Batley Variety club for £4,000 per week. The Rolls-Royce was provided by the club.

Louis Armstrong, the renowned jazz trumpeter, arrived at Yeadon Airport on 15 June 1968. He was met by Enrico Tomasso, aged 7, of York Road, Leeds, playing *Basin Street Blues* with his father Ernie. Louis was appearing with his All Stars at Batley Variety club.

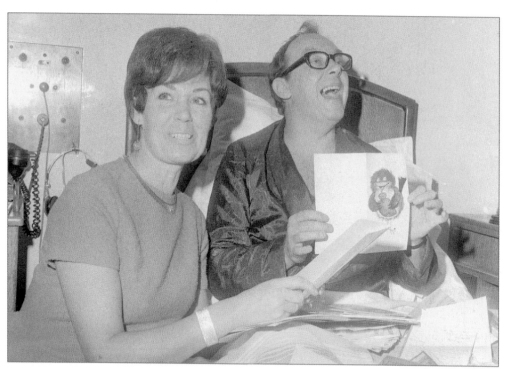

Eric Morecambe photographed in the Brotherton wing at Leeds General Infirmary, with his wife Joan, 21 November 1968. Two weeks after his heart attack he was well on the way to a full recovery and revelling in the get well cards.

Bob Monkhouse, the comedian, opened the Fine Fare supermarket at Moortown on 13 March 1969.

The Scaffold, the popular singing group, visited BBC Radio Leeds to judge a singing dogs competition on 20 February 1969. Formed in Liverpool in 1962 by the poet Roger McGough, the humorist John Gorman and the musician Mike McGear (Paul McCartney's brother), the group had big hits with *Thank U Very Much* (1967) and *Lily the Pink* (1968).

Cilla Black at Yorkshire Television studios, Kirkstall, sporting her new nose, 14 June 1969. Also present were Lionel Blair and Bruce Forsyth.

The Right Hon. Barbara Castle MP, First Secretary of State, and Alderman Major J.H. Hudson, leader of West Riding County Council, took tea together after she opened Garforth Comprehensive School, now the Community College, on 11 October 1969. Also present was County Alderman Mrs L.I. Fitzpatrick JP, Chairman of the West Riding Education Committee. There was some criticism of the cost of providing this refreshment. Although slightly out of focus this print has its own atmosphere.

Susannah York in her dressing-room at the Grand Theatre, Leeds, 18 November 1963. She was appearing in a new play, *Wings of the Dove*, adapted from Henry James's novel. She played Milly Teal, a young heiress in Venice, alongside Wendy Hiller. The production was later to go on to the West End.

Natasha Pyne and Richard Beckinsale in Shakespeare's *Romeo and Juliet*. They appeared for a photo-call at Leeds Playhouse on 1 February 1972. The Playhouse was opened on 11 December 1970 by Prince Charles as a community-based repertory theatre and is now the West Yorkshire Playhouse, Quarry Hill.

PLACES IN THE NEWS

Queens Hotel in City Square nearing completion in 1937. The hotel was rebuilt to improve travel facilities in Leeds by providing over 200 rooms, each with private bath and telephone, as well as numerous private suites, two banqueting halls accommodating 600 and 150 people respectively, a French restaurant, an American Bar, a popular-priced brasserie, a grill room and a suite of private dining rooms. However, this building was only part of the major investment of some £750,000 by the London, Midland & Scottish and London North Eastern Railway companies to improve conditions for travellers. The separate Wellington and New stations were combined to form the new Leeds Central station.

Surveying the building work before laying the foundation stones for Queens Hotel on 7 October 1936 are, left to right: Sir Josiah Stamp, LMS chairman, the lord mayor (Alderman P.T. Leigh), Lord Derby, the town clerk of Leeds, and Sir Edwin Airey, the contractor.

Harewood House, probably in the summer of 1939. This imposing house has been the home of the Lascelles family for 200 years. Built by John Carr of York between 1759 and 1771, it has spectacular interiors by Robert Adam and furniture by Thomas Chippendale. The house was remodelled to Victorian taste by Charles Barry in the 1840s. The photograph shows the south front with the terrace garden which was created between 1846 and 1850. During the war the garden was used for vegetable production and has only recently been restored.

St George's Church, 15 February 1962. Gale damage had rendered the steeple unstable. Three massive pinnacles were torn from the spire and plunged though the roof, damaging the interior. As the church was not insured against storm damage a £20,000 appeal was launched to cover the repairs. The steeple had to be removed.

Leeds bus station was re-opened by the lord mayor, Alderman E.J. Wooler, on 30 September 1963 after £66,000 had been spent on its rebuilding. Mr S. Murphy, inspector, and Mrs Margaret Ferguson, conductress, stand in a shelter in their new dark green uniforms.

City House with the old City station booking office before demolition, 1 February 1964. An extensive reconstruction project was undertaken to close Central station, rebuild City station and provide Leeds with a single, centrally sited main passenger terminal. The total cost was £4.5 million and the work was not completed until 17 May 1967.

Leeds City station before the remodelling, 1 April 1963. Steam engine class BR S, 4-6-0 type, no. 73162, was photographed leaving the station by George Williamson, who worked with Jimmie Waite during almost the whole life of the firm of Photopress (Leeds). He was interested in technical subjects while Jimmie preferred sporting events and press work.

Mill Hill Unitarian Chapel 'thought for the week', City Square, 6 January 1965. The board reads 'Some men will redevelop anything except themselves'. The site being developed was for Royal Exchange House. Interestingly, the site on the other side of the chapel, no 1 Park Row, is being redeveloped after less than thirty years.

The original site of Marks & Spencer's first stall, which stood in Leeds City Market, Kirkgate, in the 1880s, photographed on 9 December 1964. The market was burned down in 1975 and internally remodelled.

Vivian Nicholson's house, Garforth Cliff, Garforth, 16 November 1965. She had won the pools in 1961 (see p. 65) but was friendly towards the press. Despite having requested privacy on the entry coupon she and her husband had been persuaded to allow publicity. She moved to this house after her husband had died in a car crash but stayed less than a year.

A no-entry, buses only system was introduced in Leeds at the junction of Woodhouse Lane and the Headrow, now Dortmund Square. Lewis's store is on the right and Dutson's petrol station and showrooms in the background. This was one element in the 'Leeds Approach' to traffic management in an effort to improve the speed of city bus services. The photograph was taken on 6 January 1966.

Alderman A. King opened the new computer room in Civic Hall, Leeds, 22 February 1966. The labour leader switched on the new ICT computer which was to prepare over 100,000 rate accounts and 10,000 wage and salary details.

Tea in the Tunnel, 14 June 1966. This unlikely location was used for a special tea party for members of the Cement Association on a visit to inspect the Inner Ring Road construction under Woodhouse Lane. As part of the 'Leeds Approach' to tackling future traffic problems the road system was improved by placing major new roads in cuttings to avoid disfiguring the appearance of the city.

Wool Industries Research Association, Torridon, Headingley Lane, 3 October 1963. Founded in 1918, the Association was funded by a statutory levy on the wool textile industry and a new wool carding machine was installed. The buildings were demolished once WIRA left and the site is now occupied by Bass North.

PEOPLE IN THE NEWS

*On 27 September 1961 Keith Howard Nicholson, a
Castleford miner, and his wife Vivian left Leeds on the
7.30 a.m. train for London to collect a cheque for
£152,319 from Bruce Forsyth on behalf of Littlewood's
Pools. (This was equivalent to winning over a million
pounds today.) Vivian announced memorably she was going
to 'spend, spend, spend!'*

The funeral procession of 2nd Lt. Anthony Moorhouse, 10 January 1957. He was kidnapped and murdered in Egypt during the Suez Crisis. His coffin was borne on a gun carriage from St Anne's Cathedral to Lawnswood Cemetery, accompanied by members of the West Riding Regiment and attended by warrant officers and sergeant majors from 'D' Company. Walking behind the carriage are Lt. Moorhouse's father Frank and younger brother Peter. This funeral had a great impact on the whole population of the city.

Monks at Kirkstall Abbey, 9 July 1950. A group of the Passionist Fathers from Ilkley came for the special service held at the Abbey to celebrate Holy Year and the centenary of the restoration of the Roman Catholic Hierarchy.

Irene Smith, aged 15, of Beeston County Primary
School, as Leeds Children's Day Queen, 6 May
1948. She was photographed with the radio
personality Wilfrid Pickles, one of the judges, on
the steps of Leeds Civic Hall. Children's Day was
last held in 1963.

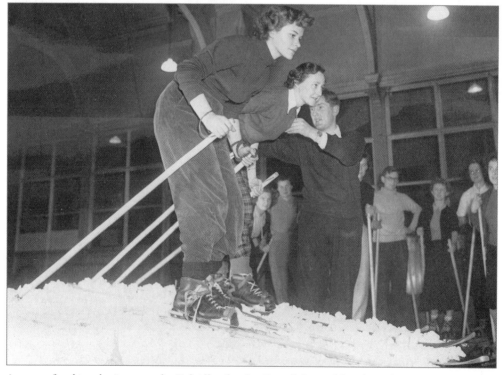

A course for ski enthusiasts, run by Ted Allen for the Central Council for Physical Recreation, was held
on the top floor of a Leeds school. This photograph, taken on 23 February 1954, shows Valerie Robinson,
aged 17, and Barbara Kendall, aged 24, practising for a trip to Norway in March.

The artist Jacob Kramer painting the portrait of Miss B. Morrit of Menston, 1 March 1961. Born in the Ukraine in 1892, this was one of his last commissions before his death on 3 February 1962.

These three ladies, with 150 years' service between them, retired from Horsforth Steam Laundry on 7 March 1962.

Reg Rosindale was the first person to 'borrow a picture' under the new lending scheme begun by Leeds Art Gallery on 11 December 1961. He borrowed the watercolour 'Dieppe Harbour', painted by John Cotman in 1823 and valued in 1961 at £50. This painting is now considered too valuable to be included in the scheme.

Railway porter Jack Cornwall retired at Bramley railway station after eight years, on 21 November 1962. Previously he had been the leader of a symphony orchestra and was known locally as 'the Music Man'.

Aileen Duffield of The Green, Guiseley, a student of Hammersmith Art College, then at Leeds College of Art, tried her hand at snow-sculpting. She produced this masterpiece 'Eskimo Nell'. Someone rang the local press who took pictures but did not publish them because they thought it was 'too rude'. The comment on the negative sheet was 'not too rude for us, just too late'!

Women wrestling at Kirkstall, 4 April 1963. Susan Moore (left) fights Ann Deering.

Dunlop and Ranken, Leeds, steel stockists and constructional engineers. This secretary retired on 29 May 1963 after working for the firm for forty-three years. The firm was founded by John Dunlop in 1911 and was bought by George Cohen, Sons & Co. (600 Group) in 1956.

Methley miners after a sit-down strike at Savile pit bottom, 19 September 1963. They were demanding extra pay for working an unusually difficult face and came up after three days when the management agreed to discuss their grievance. Among the eighteen coal-fillers were Mark Walker, Harry Johnson, Jimmy Gee and Clifford Owens.

Pickets outside the Plaza Cinema, Upper Briggate, 8 October 1963. They were objecting to the Italian film *Mondo Cane*, or was it just a publicity stunt? Despite hostile critical reaction, this first film in the 'shockumentary' genre was a huge commercial success.

Ria Roeber, a Dutch trapeze artist, swinging from a crane 100 ft above Merrion Street, Leeds, 16 December 1963. This was a publicity stunt for Billy Smart's Circus.

David Bruce MacDougall, aged 11, of Chapel Allerton demonstrated initiative in sending his plans for the Channel Tunnel to the Minister of Transport. The Minister, Ernest Marples MP, was very impressed. The boy was photographed with his plans on 2 December 1963.

Richard Ormesher of Moseley Wood Gardens, Cookridge, already a jigsaw expert at the age of 3, photographed on 27 March 1964.

Mrs Marjorie Ziff, wife of the chairman of Town Centre Securities Ltd, opened the £6 million Merrion Centre on 26 May 1964. She was presented with a golden key to open a gilded cage containing a huge cake modelled on the shopping centre, which was described by the *Yorkshire Evening Post* as 'the shape of things to come in every big town or city'.

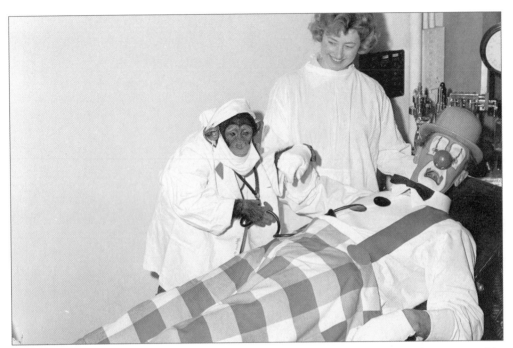

Spuggy, the clown at Billy Smart's Christmas Circus, being treated by Knoble the chimp, assisted by Daphne Murgatroyd, an assistant at Leeds General Infirmary, 12 December 1964. Spuggy was a theatre technician at the LGI before becoming a clown.

Dr J. Sweetman, Director of Temple Newsam, photographed on 1 September 1965 with the desk made by Thomas Chippendale for the library at Harewood House and purchased for £43,050. This was a world record price for English furniture at auction.

Sir William Carron, Chairman of the Trades Union Congress, opened the offices of the Amalgamated Engineering Union in Bridge Street on 11 October 1965. The building now houses a department of Park Lane College.

Jimmy Savile, former miner and ballroom manager with Mecca, became a radio disc jockey and television personality with regular appearances on *Top of the Pops* from 1960 onwards. He favoured an occasional change of appearance. Here he had his hair dyed in two tones, possibly at Muriel Smith's in Commercial Street, 14 December 1965.

Four Leeds police marriages. From front to back: PC Michael Turner and his wife, WPC Christine Turner after five months of marriage; PC Gerald Ingham and WPC Evelyn Ingham after two months; PC Michael Shires and WPC Elaine Shires after four months; and Sergeant Peter Spence and WPC Margaret Spence, after 17 months. They were photographed outside the new Westgate headquarters on 9 February 1966.

Suffragettes at Abbey House Museum, 29 February 1966. Mrs Lorna Cohen of Leeds was at the opening of the exhibition 'Votes for Women' along with other former suffragettes from London.

The 7th Earl of Harewood, photographed when he became President of Leeds United Football Club at Elland Road, 2 March 1966.

Milk Race, Roundhay, 28 June 1966. The stage prize in the 15th Tour of Britain was presented by Alderman J.S. Walsh, Lord Mayor of Leeds. The first Tour took place in 1951 but it was not until 1958 that the Milk Marketing Board took over the promotion.

Alan Holliday, Leeds Town Crier, 20 April 1967. He was employed by the Merrion Centre in what was believed to be the first full-time post in Britain. His job was to shout out every hour snippets of local and national news and shopping information. This photograph also shows the Centre before the roof was added over the pedestrian areas.

Joan Morton, butcher, 18 April 1967. She had worked in her father's pork butcher's shop in Burley since leaving school.

Girls who were to compete to announce the first programme on BBC Radio Leeds on 24 June, photographed on 12 April 1968. One of a chain of thirty-seven stations in England, Radio Leeds was the result of a long campaign by Frank Gillard, who had been impressed with the value of local radio in the USA in the 1950s. The BBC, with the support of Leeds City Council, opened the studio in the Merrion Centre. The service moved to Woodhouse Lane in 1978.

Alan Ayckbourn, the country's most successful living playwright, photographed at home in Seacroft with his sons, Philip and Steven, 7 February 1969. At this time he was drama producer for BBC North Region at Leeds. His first commercial success had been with *Relatively Speaking* in 1967; perhaps they are reading drafts of his next West End production, *How the Other Half Loves*, staged in 1970.

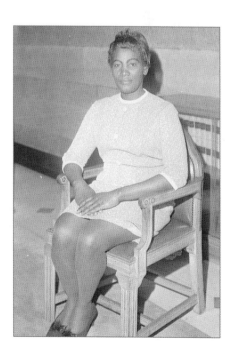

Mrs Dianna Phillip of Harehills, photographed on 29 April 1969. She was the first black Justice of the Peace to be sworn in. Originally from St Kitts, she was married with six children.

Former lord mayors at Leeds Civic Hall, 5 May 1969. Eleven former lord mayors and four former aldermen were elected Honorary Aldermen and met to sign the Roll of Aldermen. Front row, left to right: Hon. Ald. D.G. Cowling, Hon. Ald. H. Watson, Hon. Ald. H. Spink, Lord Mayor J. Rafferty, Hon. Ald. H.S. Vick, Hon. Ald. S. Hand, Hon. Ald. J.S. Walsh. Centre row: Hon. Ald. Mrs G.H. Stevenson, Hon. Ald. Mrs L. Hammond, Hon. Ald. Mrs L. Naylor, Hon. Ald. Mrs M. Pearce, Hon. Ald. Mrs M. Happold, Hon. Ald. Miss E.M. Lister. Back row: Mr E. Egan (mace-bearer), Mr N.C. Haslegrave, Hon. Ald. E.J. Wooler, Hon. Ald. T.A. Jessop, Hon. Ald. Sir James Croysdale.

Leeds West Indian Carnival at the Mecca Ballroom, Merrion Centre, 27 August 1970. Miss Jean Jeffers was presented and crowned by the previous year's Carnival Queen, Miss Janet France. Her costume was called 'Caribbean Sky at Night'.

BUSINESSES IN THE NEWS

Littlewood Store, Briggate, Leeds, was re-opened on 21 May 1970 after rebuilding. During the ceremony store manager Robert Bruce watched Miss Andrea Dowson, a sales assistant, present Alderman Arthur Brown, Lord Mayor of Leeds, with an onyx deskset inscribed to commemorate the opening of the store. 'Miss Littlewood', Miss Ida Bailey, was on the right. She was an executive secretary with Littlewoods Pools Division, Liverpool.

Coopers at Tetleys Brewery, 6 May 1960. A coopering apprentice celebrates his coming of age and the completion of his 'time' at Tetleys Brewery. The traditional practice was to burn the shavings from the apprentice's last barrel, mix it up into a disgusting 'soup' with water and pour it over the apprentice after putting him in the barrel. The barrel was then rolled about and spun around for a while.

The directors of Montague Burton Ltd, tailors, at Harrogate, 22 November 1960. Left to right: R.M. Burton, L. Jacobson (Chairman), R. Burton, J. Whitehouse, S.H. Burton, H.V. Evans, A.R. Nunns, A.J. Burton, H.E. Thirsk. Founded in around 1908 by Montague Burton, the firm became a public company in 1929 but was dominated by the founder until his death in 1952.

Time for a tea-break at Joseph May & Son (Leeds) Ltd, clothing manufacturers, Whitehall Road, Holbeck, 29 September 1961. The firm was begun by a woollen merchant in 1859 and became a significant producer of ready-to-wear men's clothing under the brand name 'Maenson'. This photograph and the one below were taken at a time when tea-breaks were said to be adversely affecting the productivity of British business.

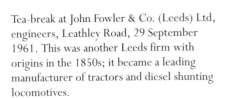

Tea-break at John Fowler & Co. (Leeds) Ltd, engineers, Leathley Road, 29 September 1961. This was another Leeds firm with origins in the 1850s; it became a leading manufacturer of tractors and diesel shunting locomotives.

Schoolgirls at a fashion show staged for them at the Metropole Hotel by Messrs Hey & Flockton Ltd, dress makers, of Marshall Mills, Holbeck, 15 May 1963.

Firing a flare at Yeadon Airport to frighten the seagulls away to assist the landing of aircraft, 1 May 1962. The Leeds/Bradford Airport was opened in 1931 and was requisitioned by the Air Ministry during the war. It was not handed back to the joint local authorities of Leeds and Bradford until 1959.

This copy of Queen Fabiola's dress, exclusively retailed by John Barry in Leeds and Bradford, was modelled at the Metropole Hotel in aid of the British Empire Cancer Campaign on 30 August 1963. The original was worn at a state banquet given for the King and Queen of Belgium in May. Created by Jacques Heim of Paris for £40,000, it was made of white satin entirely embroidered with pearls and other coloured stones.

Interior of Leeds Casino, 4 January 1964. Casinos and betting shops began to spring up all over the country after the passing of the Betting and Gambling Act 1960. The first casino in Yorkshire was opened in Mexborough in August 1962. Bingo became a popular pastime as a result and provided a new use for redundant cinemas.

Another circus publicity stunt, 2 January 1965. The strong-man from Billy Smart's Circus pulled a Leeds City Transport bus loaded with passengers with his teeth. Quarry Hill Flats can be seen in the background.

Midland Bank, 25A Park Square West, 15 October 1964. The bank kept this branch open for just over ten years. The building now houses the Kingston Unity Friendly Society.

Polar bears at the offices of British European Airways, 32 The Headrow, 21 August 1964. They were to take part in the zoo exhibition across the road at Schofields.

Schofields' zoo exhibition, held on the roof of the store at 79 The Headrow on 25 August 1964, was part of a major exhibition staged to attract families to the store.

The 24 ft horizontal tandem compound cylinder steam engine at Bean Ing Mill, Wellington Street, 9 January 1965. Built by Woodhouse and Mitchell of Brighouse, this engine, named 'Gladstone', was the largest in the mill and dated from around 1888. Nominally 40 hp but probably capable of ten times that figure, it was eventually broken up for scrap. The blackboard behind the engine records the final stop at 4.30 p.m. on Friday 4 June 1963. The *Yorkshire Post* building now stands on the site.

The Duke of Devonshire opening the Merrion Hotel, 12 January 1966. It was the first new hotel to be built in Leeds for thirty years. Left to right: John Davis (Chairman, Rank Organisation), the Duke, Alderman and Mrs W.R. Hargrave (Lord Mayor and Lady Mayoress of Leeds).

Associated British Picture Corporation TV offices at Permanent House, The Headrow, Leeds, 8 June 1966. The company brought independent television to Yorkshire on 3 November 1956 and provided programmes for the North and Midlands at weekends.

Lorries built by Yorkshire Patent Steam Wagons Ltd, Hunslet, awaiting export to Chile, 2 November 1965.

Topping out – builders celebrating the completion of the roof structure at the new Royal Exchange House, City Square, 8 February 1966. The workers were given free drinks.

The Original Oak bowling club of Headingley played a centenary bowls match against Tetley's representatives on 1 June 1968. Miss Joan Parton of Headingley wore a mini dress which was in striking contrast to the other players who were dressed in period costume.

A performance of *The Good Old Days* at Leeds City Varieties, Swan Street, 7 May 1967. Filmed in the theatre, the popular BBC Television production became TV's longest running music show, and ran from 1953 to 1983.

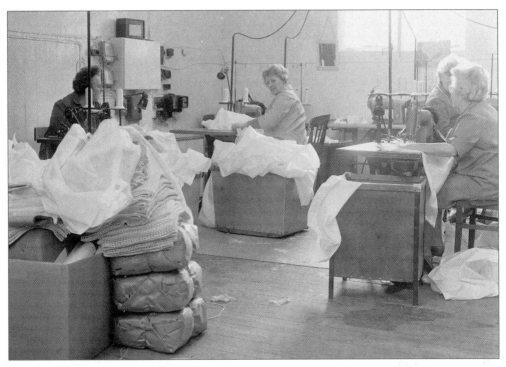

The machine room at the Moor Road Works of James Spencer Ltd, Headingley, 13 November 1968. Sewing laundry bags are, left to right: Mrs Atherley, Mrs Wormald, Mrs Spurdon and Mrs Estell. The firm became a limited company in 1949 and expanded into hospital supplies. It has recently relocated to Prospect Mills, Wilsden, Bradford.

The Hunslet Engine Company's steam engine *Bahamas* after reconditioning, 11 March 1968. This company only went public in the early 1960s although locomotives had been built on the site since 1839. The company concentrated on diesel locomotives, producing a range of models from small mining locomotives to the heaviest railway units.

Forging brake drums with a drop hammer at Kirkstall Forge, England's oldest ironworks, which claims over 750 years of almost continuous operation, 14 May 1969. Iron ceased to be worked in 1920 and the firm concentrated on the axle side of the business. In the 1960s they were one of the leading makers of heavy steel drop forgings and were prominent as producers of high grade carbon and alloy bright steel bars, but they were most widely known for making axles for commercial vehicles. The works was recently sold by GKN to the Dana Corporation of the USA and is now known as Spicer Axles, Kirkstall.

Directors of Jonas Woodhead & Sons Ltd, spring manufacturers, Kirkstall Road, 18 June 1969. Left to right: Deputy Chairman Stanley Markland, Chairman Peter B. Higgins and General Managing Director Ernest S. Simpson. Originating in Bradford, the firm moved to Leeds at the turn of the century and became a public limited company in 1935.

Mr Wheatley's rhubarb sheds at Carlton, Rothwell, 16 January 1969. Jimmie Waite was related to the Wheatleys on his mother's side of the family. They had earlier operated a market garden at Scott Hall.

The cleaner Queenie Fields opened the £80,000 factory for John Waddington (Games Division) at Woodlesford on 10 December 1969. The managing director Victor Watson is standing on her left. The printing, games and packaging company was founded in the 1890s and sold its games interests to Hasbro in 1994.

Tailors on strike, Woodhouse Moor, with St Marks School in the background, 25 February 1970. Five thousand clothing factory workers rejected the offer of immediate negotiations on their claim if they returned to work. Charlie Taylor was chairman of the unofficial strike committee.

Primrose Hill Colliery, Swillington, after closure, 6 March 1970. George Prince, the colliery manager, together with his under manager C. Shaw and training officer Jack Kielty, had a drink with the miners who worked the last shift. The previous week the pit had broken the record for production. Its closure was marked with barrels of free beer for the miners.

Miners at Robin Hood Colliery, Rothwell, collecting concessionary coal, 8 January 1972. Children helped their parents to fill sacks as miners collected orders that were up to six weeks overdue as the result of an overtime ban. A national pit strike was due to begin at midnight and this was their last chance to pick up fuel before it began. There was a mile long queue to the depot.

SECTION ELEVEN

SPORT

*Don Revie, the most successful manager in the history of
Leeds United Football Club, photographed at the Elland
Road ground on 29 April 1969. He is holding telegrams
congratulating him on his team winning the League
Championship by a record 67 points. Jimmie Waite enjoyed
the sporting environment and was good at sports
photography. The considerable demand for good football
and cricket prints made Saturdays the busiest day of the
week since there were weddings in the mornings and
generally several sporting events in the afternoon. At least
two photographers were needed to cover both ends of a pitch
and to take film back to the dark room for immediate
processing for the early evening editions of local
newspapers. They also aimed at the national Sunday
newspapers including the* Sunday Express *and the* News
of the World, *and Monday morning editions of national
daily newspapers.*

Yorkshire County Cricket team, 1957. Back row, left to right: K. Taylor, J.G. Binks, D.E.V. Padgett, R. Appleyard, F.S. Truman, M.J. Cowan, R. Illingworth. Front row: J.V. Wilson, W. Watson, W.H.H. Sutcliffe, J.H. Wardle, F.A. Lowson. In that year Yorkshire finished third in the Championship. This was a proof print annotated by Jimmie Waite. The firm published a popular series of team photographs in postcard form.

Groundsman Arthur Waite preparing the notorious Headingley pitch for the forthcoming Test match against New Zealand, 27 June 1958. In this (Third) Test New Zealand made their lowest ever innings total of 67 after heavy rain. Although planned for 3–8 July, there was no play on 3 or 4 July because of the rain. England won by an innings and 71 runs. Ray Illingworth made his Test debut in this match.

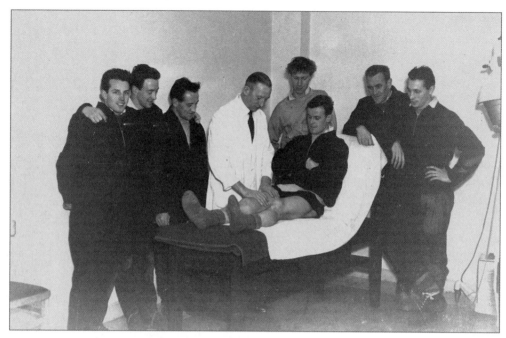

Leeds United footballers during training at Elland Road, 3 December 1958. Shackleton receives treatment on the couch, while among those looking on are Humphries, Cush, Charlton, Revie and Gibson. Don Revie had made his debut as a Leeds player on 28 November, in a 3–2 win over Newcastle.

Motorcycle scrambling, otherwise called Motocross, on Otley Chevin, 2 November 1961. This was a stock shot by George Williamson.

Edwards of Warrington was unable to stop Ratcliffe, the Leeds winger, from scoring in the Rugby league match at Headingley on 7 October 1961. Jimmie entered this action shot for the British Press Pictures competition but does not appear to have won. The match was notable for thirty-four penalties. The *Yorkshire Evening Post* commented that 'if [the referee] had whistled every time the laws were broken goodness only knows what would have happened'. The final score was Leeds 10 Warrington 9.

Leeds United vs. Norwich, 28 September 1963. Keelan, the Norwich goalkeeper, could only watch as Weston (out of picture) hammered the ball into the net to score United's third goal. Thurlow of Norwich is behind Keelan. This was a typical action shot taken without the advantage of a telephoto lens.

Leeds United goalkeepers Gary Sprake (right) and Brian Williamson at Elland Road on 24 January 1966. They had just heard that they had drawn Chelsea away in the fourth round of the FA Cup. The thumbs-up sign is one of the sport's well-worn photographic conventions.

The West Indian cricket squad after winning the Fourth Test at Headingley by 221 runs on 30 July 1963. Back row, left to right: Joseph Solomon, Basil Butcher, William Rodriguez, David Allan, Derryk Murray; centre: Seymour Nurse, Launcelot Gibbs, Charles Griffiths, Lester King, Michael Carew, Easton McMorris. Front row: Albert Valentine, Conrad Hunte, Frank M. Worrell, Garfield Sobers, Wesley Hall, Rohan Kanhai.

Farokh Engineer, the Indian test cricketer, in the nets at Headingley, 7 June 1967. The First Test was played on 8–13 June, and England won by six wickets. The stand of 168 between Engineer and Wadekar was the first hundred partnership of the tour and was India's highest for the second wicket against England.

Headingley cricket ground, 2 August 1967. This stock shot from the north enclosure shows, from left to right, the Yorkshire County Cricket Club offices and dressing rooms, the Bowling Green Stand, the Leeds Pavilion and Pavilion Stand, and the Main Stand.

Yorkshire County Cricket team, 21 April 1967. Back row, left to right: G.A. Cope, P.J. Sharpe, A.G. Nicholson, P. Stringer, J.S. Waring, J.H. Hampshire, G. Boycott. Front row: D.E.V. Padgett, J.G. Binks, F.S. Truman, D.B. Close, R. Illingworth, K. Taylor, D. Wilson. In 1967 Yorkshire again won the Championship by beating Gloucestershire at Harrogate, having won it in 1960, 1962, 1963 and 1966. They were to win again the following year.

The England Rugby League test team at Parkside, Hunslet, 14 October 1963. Back row, left to right: Paddy Armour (trainer), Measures, Tenby, Bowman, Field, Tyson, Sagar, Burgess. Front row: Bolton, Gowers, Karalius, Ashton, Murphy, Fox, Bill Fallowfield (Rugby League Secretary).

A civic reception was staged at Leeds Town Hall on 8 May 1964 to celebrate Leeds United Football Club winning the Second Division Championship Cup and the West Riding Senior Cup. They were the first major trophies the team had won for forty years. Three thousand supporters in the crowd sang the *Leeds United Calypso*.

Ronnie Hilton with Leeds United footballers in the recording studio, 15 April 1964. Their record, the *Leeds Calypso*, was later released as a single.

Ray Illingworth in his garden at Farsley, 14 June 1966. He had just been picked to play for England in the Second Test against the West Indies at Lords.

Billy Bremner, the most successful captain in the history of Leeds United Football club, leaving Elland Road, 11 March 1967. He had just been declared fit to play in the fifth round of the FA Cup against Sunderland. He joined the rest of the squad at a crucial time and took them through two replays before they finally won at Hull 2–1. The second match at Elland Road attracted 57,892 spectators, the biggest crowd for thirty-five years; sadly, thirty-two of them were injured when a barrier collapsed.

Leeds United football team, 22 July 1968. Back row, left to right: P. Madeley, M. O'Grady, D. Harvey, G. Sprake, J. Charlton, N. Hunter, Don Revie. Centre row: A. Johanneson, R. Belfitt, M. Jones, T. Hibbitt, E. Gray, P. Lorimer. Front row: P. Reaney, T. Cooper, J. Giles, B. Bremner, J. Greenhoff, M. Bates. This was the team that in 1968 won the Football League Cup.

The National Cyclo-cross Championships were held in the grounds of Temple Newsam House on 29 January 1972. The sport had been gaining in popularity since 1950, and in the following year Britain hosted the World Championship at Crystal Palace, London.

ACCIDENTS

Exhausted Lance Ash was rescued by the Fire Brigade from the 130 ft chimney at Mark Rowlands furniture warehouse, East Street, 14 April 1964. He had been trapped for six hours while clearing bricks during demolition.

A tram car accident in the rush hour at Oakwood, 4 September 1952. A runaway tram travelling from Roundhay Park to Kirkstall Abbey crashed into the back of a Headingley-bound tram. Fifteen people were injured.

The story goes that one day in 1950 George Williamson was rushing to a job in Edith Waite's car and slid in the wet conditions into Calverley Bridge on the ring-road. Not one to miss an opportunity, George took a number of photographs of the accident.

A Gas Board van collided with a Leeds City Transport bus in Hunslet Road on 17 February 1963. Three men were trapped in the van.

On 10 August 1961 a Scarborough train full of holiday-makers collided with a large diesel engine and was derailed on Lower Briggate rail bridge. One man was killed, and a woman and two children were injured.

A single-engined Auster belonging to the Territorial Army Flying Group was caught in a snowstorm soon after taking off from Yeadon Airport and crashed at Guiseley, killing the pilot and two young passengers, 3 March 1962.

This lorry fell down a hole in the road during construction of the inner ring-road, September 1964.

Collision between a bus and a crane in Briggate, 29 December 1965. The crane was being used to excavate a subway at the junction with Boar Lane when the jib sliced into the upper deck of the bus. Nobody was hurt.

Jack Charlton's sports shop, in Roundhay Road, Harehills, on fire, 12 December 1970. Jack played for Leeds United for more than ten years and was Footballer of the Year in 1967.

During the afternoon of 14 April 1967, fire broke out at Rycrofts Ltd, on the corner of Briggate and Call Lane. Staff were trapped on the upper floor and three people were injured.

Sixteen people were injured when a lorry transporting a 45 ft long girder from premises in Jack Lane collided with a Middleton-bound No. 3 Leeds Corporation bus in Dewsbury Road, Hunslet, on 18 January 1966.

A serious fire broke out at the Call Lane warehouse of W. Matthewson & Co. Ltd on 28 March 1966. Built for the Aire and Calder Canal Company in 1827, the warehouse was gutted in the fire. Some £100,000-worth of wool tops, 3,000 bales of raw wool and 100 bales of hides were also destroyed.